ADEBO TOMOMEWO

POWER
OF
COMMUNION
FOR TOTAL HEALTH

ANAKTISI PUBLISHING HOUSE

Power of communion for total health
Copyright © 2016 by Adebo Tomomewo

Published by
Anaktisi Publishing House
2 Hospital Way
Hither Green
Lewisham
LONDON
SE13 6UF

All Scripture quotations are taken from the *King James* version of the Bible

All rights reserved. No part of this publication may be reproduced, stored in a retrieval system, or transmitted in any from or by any means, mechanical, electronic, photocopying or otherwise without the prior written consent of the copyright owner.

ISBN: 978-1908845-04-7

Cover and layout design
by Kotelnykova Olena
Printed in the United Kingdom

CONTENTS

Acknowledgement 7
Introduction... 8

CHAPTER 1
Divine health is your
greatest blessing • 11

CHAPTER 2
God's Provision for our health • 16

CHAPTER 3
Expect the supernatural
in your health •..................................... 21

CHAPTER 4
Signs and Wonders
in the Communion • 26

CHAPTER 5
The Two Elements of the Holy
Communion - Blood and Flesh • 28

CHAPTER 6
Testimonies •... 56

Dedication

This book is dedicated to the blessed Holy Spirit my helper and my wife Pastor (Mrs) Hyelazira Tomomewo.

Acknowledgement

The birth of a book can be likely to the birth of a new born baby,hence you cannot bring forth a child without the contributions mid - wives and nurses,so there destiny mid-Wives that me helps to bring forth this book,the first personality I want to acknowledge is My father God,my saviour Jesus and the wonderful Holy Spirit for the inspiration to write this book,I also want to appreciate my family for giving me the right atmosphere to write this book that I have been putting together for the past fours years,particularly my wife was very instrumental in getting me the materials I needed to write this book and she personally keep encouraging me to complete this book and also am concluding this book on the month of September the month that we celebrating 20years in marriage. Thank my dear wife for your constant support at different levels for me to carry out my destiny assignment.

I must not fail to mention the role of Brother Igor Kotelnikov that help me in producing this book and I also want to appreciate Rev. K. E. Tiemo for helping me to proof read this manuscript hence making the book readable to everyone. You are loved and appreciated sir.

Introduction

It is the right of every blood bought child of God to enjoy good health in the kingdom of God. *(3 John 2)*. This is to establish the will of God concerning your health, because faith starts where the will of God is known concerning any area of life but this faith comes by hearing the word *(Romans10:17)*. I'm therefore bringing to you in this book the Word of faith concerning what Jesus our physician prescribed for our total health, the Holy Communion – *John 6:48-58*, which is the eating of his body and drinking of his blood - *(Matthew 26:26-29)*.

So why did I write this book? I'm writing this book because the Lord has burdened my heart with the burden of his Heart; he was speaking to my heart from the book of *Jeremiah 8:21*.

Jeremiah 8:21…..I Am Hurt.

The Lord is saying he is concerned about the health of his people; why are they sick?

Jeremiah8:22 Is there no balm in Gilead; is there no physician there? Why then is not the health of the daughter of my people recovered?

So, in this book, am introducing to you the Holy

Communion as the balm in Gilead ordained for the recovery of your total health. This is the physician's prescription for our health.

One of the principal works of a true and good physician is the giving of right prescription to the patient and the moment you take the medication you are on your way to the recovery of your health. It therefore means that the Holy Communion is the all purpose medication for our health.

So, the kingdom provision that Christ the Physician left for us to enhance our total health is the Holy Communion. This is one of the mysteries of the kingdom that Jesus taught us while he was on earth, even though this mystery has its foundation in the Old Testament which is what we saw in *Exodus 12* where it was referred to as the Passover meal. Here we see the chains of events and miracles that took place the moment the Jews partook of this Passover meal. This was God's last card that broke the back of Pharaoh's resistance to their freedom *(Exodus12:31-33)*.

If the blood of an animal would unlock all these miracles for the Jews in Egypt, how much more miracles would New Testament believers experience in their lives when they eat the body of Jesus and drink his blood *(John 6:53-54)*.

Partaking of the Holy Communion with an

understanding of its nutritional content is what unlocks the power of this mystery for your total health, because as you take the Holy Communion you are partaking of his divine life and the divine life of Jesus carries his divine health. This is the understanding I am unveiling in this book.

As you read this book, I see this mystery of the Holy Communion terminate every misery you might be going through now in Jesus' name, because the blood of Jesus dissolves all Satan's legal rights of ownership over our lives *(Colossians 1:14).*

As you eat his body and drink his blood daily, I see everything trying to eat up your health eaten and swallowed up by the Holy Communion to establish your dominion, in Jesus' name.

Finally, I speak as one sent from heaven with a mandate to declare the recovery of destinies of people and to let them know that every one is born with a destiny. Before you finish reading this book in your hand, you shall recover your health as you put to work the understanding you will get in this book. Be blessed.

CHAPTER 1

Divine health is your greatest blessing

Next to being saved from hell and eternal destruction, divine health is the greatest blessing you can ever have. If your health fails, everything will fail with it. I'm yet to see someone, with a drip in his hands going to attend an interview. You have intelligence and you are very good mentally but you may be sick. Even when the Bible says we should praise God with all our might; you can't praise Him with any might when your might is corrupted by sickness.

I saw something very clear in Jesus ministry. Anywhere He went, He did not walk on water all the time, He did not calm the storm all the time but one thing I saw and He did all the time is, He healed. When Jesus walked on the earth, most of his miracles were in the areas of healing. There were more miracles of healing than any other kind of miracles. That shows that Healing is a very major area of concern to God. That is because it is God's nature to heal.

> *How God anointed Jesus of Nazareth with the Holy Ghost and with power: who went about doing good and healing all that were oppressed of the devil; for God was with him.*
>
> ***Acts 10:38***

Jesus is here today. How do you know He is here; because He is going to heal people today. Anywhere you see people getting healed, people sharing testimonies of being healed of varied illnesses, it is because the healer is in there *(Exodus 15:26)*. So, you don't get healing from Him; you get healing of Him; because He is the healer. You can't get the healing without the presence of the healer Himself. You can't get the fruit without the root. You don't get healing without the healer; healing is the back of the cross, Salvation is the front of the cross.

Any where you see the operation of Jesus in the Bible; it always involves healing the sick. When God brought the children of Israel out of Egypt, He brought them into the promise land. He made sure none of them was sick.

> *He brought them forth also with silver and gold: and there was not one feeble person among their tribes.*
> **Psalm 105:37**

He also saw to it that none among their tribes was feeble (sick). So, I See God fixing every feeble part of your life before you finish reading this book. There are some jobs you can't get if you are sick. Some people call off sick at work most of the time for that reason; some company will want to check how fit you are health-wise before they employ you. Some companies have some policies, if you get sick off on many occasions, they may have no choice but to lay you off from the job.

So, your health is a very major aspect that we cannot play with. You just need one part of your body to have problem then you will appreciate health. If it is your leg that has problems and you could not walk then you begin to appreciate its usefulness in your life.

I pray for you as you are reading this book, may anything not happen to any part of your body in Jesus name. Why? Because, there is no part of you that anyone will say, if it were my finger that had a problem, then it will be okay. There is no part of you that has a problem that the whole body will not pay for. That is why, God is aware of this and made provision that none among them was feeble. Just imagine, three million people no sickness; Hospitals have no jobs to do; imagine all the doctors say nobody came for check up; three million coming out of Egypt and God saw to it that they came out in health and wealthy.

There were times I watched The Exodus the Hollywood version on the TV, they show some of the old men using walking stick; they will show you some people blind in one of their eyes; that is not true. That is their own version of the Exodus; it is not the true reflection of *Psalm 105:38*.

The Biblical version of exodus says none was among them that was feeble; nobody left using stick, nobody left blind; everybody came out of Egypt fully healthy. Glory to God, None of them was sick before; but later, some fell sick because he said to them:

> *And ye shall serve the Lord your God, and he shall bless thy bread, and thy water; and I will take sickness away from the midst of thee.*
>
> **Exodus 23:25-26**

In other words, He was still saying, I will take sickness away before they left and When they were to go out of Egypt, He took it; because the journey they were going was a long one. According to God's plan, it was meant to be less than one month journey.

The journey was not on fast track train; it was not by a vehicle but they were to walk on foot. God knew they needed to be in health to get to their promise land. That means the Promise Land was not sure without a good health. For instance you may not find a life partner to marry you for lack of good health.

What I am trying to say is this; God brought three million people who came out of Egypt healed, healthy and whole. I have good news for you; God is still in that same business, he has not changed, you will walk out of this sickness troubling you now totally healed, healthy and whole in Jesus' name.

CHAPTER 2

God's Provision for our health

God made provision therefore for us to ensure that this is done; that is what we have in the partaking of the Lord's body. It is meant to bring healing; because it is in God's nature to heal his people. The Holy Communion table is a healing table. This is a table that will communicate total healing to every part of your body, since we know it is God's will to heal. Have you ever wondered why Christians are sick? I'm not talking about minor sickness like cough and cold related sicknesses, environmental sicknesses.

We know that during certain seasons, weather-wise, there are people who complain of certain sicknesses; for instance, in Europe or America during winter a lot of old people complain of Arthritis , Cold related sicknesses, Flu, etc. That is why they advertise on the TV for people to come and buy medication to sort it out. Now I'm talking about terminal diseases, life threatening illnesses.

People of the world are sick and that should

not be a surprise to you because Jesus is not the Saviour of their souls neither is he the Saviour of their body. *(Ephesians 5:23)* So they were free to be sick; no wonder many were sick. But when believers are sick continuously like the sinners I want to know why?

From Biblical conclusion, one of the reasons why believers are sick is what we are talking about in this book.

1 Corinthians gave the answer:

> *For he that eateth and drinketh unworthily, eateth and drinketh damnation to himself, not discerning the Lord's body*
> **1 Corinthians 11:29**

They were sick because they did not discern the Lord's body. For the lack of discerning the Lord's body was the reason why they were weak, sick and people were dying in the Church. When you see believers dying before their time, you need to know that something is going wrong somewhere. How can somebody be dying in their early 30 or 40 years of age.

You may say Jesus died within that age bracket. You are not Jesus, for He died at thirty three for a reason, so that you would not die young with an unfulfilled destiny. He was on a divine mission of redemption; So who are you dying for? Who will your blood save? Forty which is the apex of a man's life is not your time of death; you are just starting life at forty. How can you die even at fifty? It's an error. Sickness can hinder some people from getting to age fifty. Why is it that people are dying in the Church? It should not be so because partaking of the Body of Christ is meant to prolong your life. It's anti-death drug for the believer *(John6:50)*

So the Bible says in the case of the Corinthian Church, they did not discern the Lord's body, they did not understand the virtues resident in his body, the divine efficacy and capability of his body in a believers body, hence the Bible didn't say 'they didn't discern the Lord's blood' because there are two components when it comes to the Holy Communion.

There are two elements which are the Flesh (body) and the blood of Jesus. The Bible did not say they died because they did not discern the Lord's blood but they died because they did not discern the lord's body. What does that mean? They were weak for not understanding the content of the Holy Communion. They did not understand the sacredness; they did not understand what it carries. What it carries by revelation to you determines what it offers.

> *For I have received of the Lord that which also I delivered unto you, that the Lord Jesus the same night in which he was betrayed took bread...*
> **1 Corinthians 11:23**

Paul never met Christ physically. He was not there when Jesus was teaching them about his body. Paul said that, what he was telling them was what he received by revelation and not by information. I am teaching you now but I pray you receive a personal revelation before you come to the Holy Communion table.

When you come to the table, come with an understanding that this is not just bread or ordinary bread but come with the understanding of the content of His body that, divinity is about to enter your humanity; that way, you are discerning the Lord's body.

You are able to partake of what He carries. You are taking it with understanding of its calories. You understand the divine and spiritual forces that are inside the content of the communion.

You understand that, this is the father's prescription for our total health. There is a healing balm inside these elements. This thing can kill cancer; it can destroy arthritis; it can root out bareness. Whatever sickness that was not there in the beginning when God created you can be swallowed up by the Holy Communion. So, when you come with this kind of understanding, then you are discerning the Lord's body.

If you take it without knowing the content, you are not discerning the Lord's body. The word discerning means understanding, and that is why the Bible says, they were weak, they were sick, and they died because they did not understand the Lord's body. If you understand what these two components carry, it will change your approach to the Communion Table.

CHAPTER 3

Expect the supernatural in your health

When you take the Holy Communion today, you may not experience the spectacular but you will experience the supernatural. You may not experience some spectacular physical manifestation like something happening to you e.g. shaking or trembling, but you will experience the supernatural operation in your health.

Paul is trying to tell us to watch out when believers start dying before their time or start falling sick anyhow, when a believer starts saying I am weak or tired all the time. Any small thing this believer will say I am tired. When tiredness and weakness become their watchword, it means they do not know how to table advantage of the Holy Communion to handle that area of challenges. So, I want you to understand what the Holy Communion table carries for your total health. In other words, some people who do not understand why they are taking the Lord's body and the sacredness. Imagine somebody coming to the Holy Communion table carelessly without understanding is a proof that the person does not know the sacredness of what is on that table. Some have no understanding of what the flesh and blood of Jesus on the table is capable of.

We take it in the Church regularly to give us understanding so that you can do it at home regularly.

If you want to see manifestations, you will need to do it continually *(1Corinthians11:26)*. When you do it continually, then you will begin to see skin disease and other afflictions being destroyed. You will begin to see certain sicknesses that you have been battling with that are resistant to drugs disappears; they can't be resistant to the communion because it will tackle sickness to the roots. It's like when Jesus said to the fig tree, that from that day no man 'eat from you'. He was not shouting, he just said from today no man eats from thee any more.

What happened to that tree was not spectacular, it was supernatural. Why? It was not immediately but the following day. *(Mark 11:12-14, 20-22)*. What Jesus said happened in the physically realm later. Initially it was as if nothing happened but something began to happen in the realm of the Spirit. That is what will happen via the Holy Communion when you partake of it by faith based on the word of God.

Something will step out of the physical to the invisible realm. It will begin to take out sicknesses and diseases in your body. Get ready because supernatural things will be happening within you as you partake of the Holy Communion daily. Partaking of the Holy Communion daily is one of the ways to provoke the supernatural in your health daily; a case where the divinity packaged in body and his blood is on patrol in your own natural body to sustain and maintain your health.

So this Understanding is very important. Every undertaking becomes easy with understanding because no man lives beyond the level of his understanding. You will experience a major surge in your energy level as you partake of the Holy Communion. Something's you have never done before, you will begin to attempt and dare them now because energy and vigour have come.

People will say it is too much for you but you will say no, because you have the energy for it. God will give you some supernatural lucozade, some energy booster via the Holy Communion. When you come to the table, take it with understanding with revelation and discerning of the Lord's body. Many were sick at the time of the Church in Corinth because they could not receive the divine life of the

Saviour. So, they were weak and died prematurely. It means if we discern the Lord's body, expect to walk in health and wholeness. When you discern the Lord's body, you are drinking into health, long life and wholeness.

Having the understanding of the nutritional content of the flesh and blood of Jesus helps you know what the Holy Communion contains in terms of health, strength and long life (*1 Corinthians 11:29-30*).

Holy Communion is a key channel for health and wholeness for God's people. So know what you are walking into health and wholeness by the table.

> *And they, continuing daily with one accord in the temple, and breaking bread from house to house, did eat their meat with gladness and singleness of heart*
>
> ***Acts 2:46, 47***

This people discern the Lord's body and they therefore continue to take it continually. The bible says they took it continually; they discerned the Lord's body; they understood it; they were with the master when He said, 'take eat; this is my body'. He broke His body. They understood it, therefore, there was no much teaching. They understood how His own body functioned while he was on earth with them as his disciples. He was never down with sickness once; they saw how His body functioned without sickness and disease; they saw how He walked in the midst of dusty places and yet He was never sick once. They saw how His body functioned here and said now that you are giving us your body; it's a good one, a part exchange for our own weak body parts. Look at the verse again - *And they, continuing daily with one accord in the temple, and breaking bread from house to house, did eat their meat with gladness and singleness of heart.*

The problem I discover is not with God, the problem is with the lack of understanding of his body. *Acts2: 46*

CHAPTER 4

Signs and Wonders in the Communion

Let go back to verse 42 and 43 of the same scripture Acts 2

> *And they continued steadfastly in the apostles' doctrine and fellowship, and in breaking of bread, and in prayers. And fear came upon every soul: and many wonders and signs were done by the apostles.*
>
> ***Acts 2:42-43***

The early church had results from partaking of the Holy Communion because they were doing it daily. Signs and wonders broke loose in all the houses. If you take it with this understanding of discerning the Lord's body now and say Lord I want to be taking it as an addict, every day in our house; then get ready for signs and wonders. The bible says because they were doing it from house to house daily, there were many signs and wonders.

The key is that they continued.

They continued steadfastly in the apostle's doctrine, they continued in the breaking of bread and prayers because of the continuity and the convergence of the consistency, signs and wonders were let loose in their houses. At that time they didn't have where to gather, they were doing it in the houses.

Let's believe God that from now on, as we continue to partake of this Holy Communion daily with new belief we shall begin to hear testimonies breaking out in our houses, over our children, our marriages and the entire families.

Let's begin to treat problems that have no medical solution with this mystery; I mean the mystery of the Holy Communion. Let's begin to deal with every misery associated with our health using this kingdom mystery.

In summary, God wants to restore the true meaning and power of the Holy Communion in the Church so that His people will rightfully discern His body and release strong health and wholeness back to His body. Healing is dispensed at this table. Holy Communion will do something; it will add years to your life and it will add life also to your years.

CHAPTER 5

The Two Elements of the Holy Communion - Blood and Flesh

The communion is made up of two elements.
1. The Body – *Matthew 26:26 - 29 and Matthew 26:26.*

> *.....Jesus took the bread ......and said take, eat, this is my body*

The bread is served to us at the Holy Communion table. Jesus gave them the physical bread and said eat, so the bread is for eating. The bread by faith, was converted to his body, so every time we come to the Holy Communion table, we are taking the body of Jesus, some bread taken bread from one bakery somewhere.

Remember, Jesus said '...*Take, eat, this is my body*', not this was the body rather this is my body; present tense, so, when you take the bread, you are taking fresh every time, you partake of the Holy Communion.

Therefore, the First Element that is served at the Holy Communion table is His body which is the bread. *(1 Corinthians 11:29 - 30)*.

To discern His body means to know and understand what the bread represent; that is to say having understanding of what you are holding in your hand when you are eating. The revelation through which you are partaking of the bread is what determines its effect on your health.

For instance the body of Jesus did not come from the dust like the first Adam. Jesus' body was made from the word of God *(John1:1, 14)*. That is why, when he died, his body did not decompose like the body of a natural man If the Holy Spirit had not raised him up, the body would still be there till now, because the word of God is incorruptible; and therefore lives and abide forever *(1Peter1:23)*.

So, when you hold the bread, you are holding an incorruptible body that can swallow everything corrupting your health. When you are eating the body of Jesus you are partaking of the incorruptible in the word form hence Jesus said *'am the living bread' (John6:51),* because he also is the living word. Therefore, eating his body is taking the word made flesh for your total health; that is what made Jesus not only the saviour of our soul but also the saviour of our body *(Ephesians 5:23)* He saved you from sin, also saved your body from sickness.

When a believer dies before his time, that may be one of the reasons behind it. If a believer falls sick all the time, there is a reason behind it. If you are weak all the time, no energy, there is a reason behind it.

If this was because of not discerning the Lord's body, if you now discern the Lord's body, things should begin to change. You can discern the Lord's body and not be taking it. You can so discern the Lord's body, know all the things you need to know about it but if you don't take it, don't attend Holy Communion service the Church puts in place, sitting at home; you fall to the same class of the people that do not discern it yet they are taking it.

Some people take it but don't understand it; so as a result there is no healing; no miracle follows because they are just taking it religiously and ignorantly.

Jesus establishes it that the bread which is His body is for our healing. He said this is my body that I break for you so that your body will not be broken. I break it for your wholeness.

> *The woman was a Greek, a Syrophenician by nation; and she besought him that he would cast forth the devil out of her daugh-*

> *ter. But Jesus said unto her, let the children first be filled: for it is not meet to take the children's bread, and to cast it unto the dogs. And she answered and said unto him, Yes, Lord: yet the dogs under the table eat of the children's crumbs. And he said unto her, For this saying go thy way; the devil is gone out of thy daughter.*
>
> **Mark 7:26-28**

Healing is equated to bread here in verse 27. In other words Jesus is trying to say healing is the children's bread. If by the crumbs that fell from the table, the woman's daughter was set free from a demonic power how much more when you take the whole bread on the table? So, the divine forces within this bread can drive out devils. If a child is having demonic attack, serve him or her the Holy Communion by faith for healing; healing is for children of God and not just for everybody.

If the woman could agree that as a dog she could take the crumbs of bread for healing and deliverance, it means she was able to discern the Lord's body. Some people would have been angry for being called a dog but the woman could discern that the crumbs contained her healing.

As a result of this Jesus said to her go your way for the devil is gone out of your daughter. So the devil can go out of your business, marriage as you partake of the Holy Communion. If you have this kind of faith, the devil will be gone out of your family. If crumbs could tackle a devil, think about what the bread on the Holy Communion table will do for you.

The devil went out by the crumbs, so there is healings and also deliverance inside the bread. So as you discern the Lord's body and come before the Holy Communion table, look at any area the devil is punishing you, tell the devil to take his hands off your business, your children, etc.

If the devil is gone out with a crumb, how much more the whole bread. This is how to discern the Lord's body. Coming to the Holy Communion table without this understanding is dangerous. Wherever the devil is operational in your health, you can serve him quit notice at the Holy Communion table. If the crumbs could do it, Jesus is the same yesterday, today and forever, complete bread would do a better work for your total health.

2. The Blood

There are three levels of blood Administration. We administer the blood in three ways. This is to give you understanding of the multiple ways in which the blood operates in the life of a believer for Total Health and Victory in life

➤ *The Blood of Speaking*

This is done by pleading the blood *Revelation 12:11*. You can plead the blood over your home, your Journey, your premises, your business. This blood stand at the boundary of your life to protect you from the evil spirits, and the blood is for defensive and offensive operation in prayers.

You can draw the blood circle around your house, children, etc. You can draw the blood line in prayers and use it to cover yourself or cover the road while driving or cover the airspace while in the aircraft by faith. You can use it to rebuke the forces of hell.

➤ *The blood of Sprinkling - Hebrews 12:22-24*

Amongst other things that happen in Zion, he said, that, we have come to the blood of sprinkling. The original of this spiritual exercise was in the book of Exodus 12 when the children of Israel were to depart from Egypt after all the miracles had been done and Pharaoh would not let them go. Then God said I know what I would do, I will give the blood as the last card of victory *Exodus 12:3-23*, to be sprinkled at the top of the door post so that when the death Angel passes, he will pass over their homes.

It means therefore, the angel of death cannot penetrate where the blood is. So you can sprinkle the blood in your home, your premises, on your car or your Aircraft etc. to keep death angels off. The death Angel could kill those that had the blood on the door; the blood became their security *(Zachariah 9:15)*.

The blood is for your defense; the blood that is sprinkled is for your defense. As you sprinkle the blood on your car and journey, accident would be far away from you because the blood will stand as your stronghold *Zachariah 9:11-15*. The reason for this is that when you sprinkle the blood it speaks something better than the blood of Abel *(Hebrews 12:24)* It can speak for untimely death to Passover you and your family. We sprinkle it to deal with external spiritual forces.

If all these interventions happened in Egypt via just the blood of Lambs, how much more damage the blood of Jesus would do against the force of darkness in your life; because today Jesus is that Feast of Passover *(1 Corinthians 5:7-8)*, which is ordained for the release of the saints from satanic captivity when they are under attack *Luke 23:16-17*. Every time the blood is sprinkled by faith, people are released from Satan's captivity and oppression.

The blood when sprinkled enforced the release of 3 million Jews in one single night. As you sprinkle this blood I see you released from that satanic attack now in Jesus' name. The Anointing destroys the yoke *(Isaiah 10:27)* but the blood of Jesus destroys the yoker (the personality behind the yoke) and release you from your captor.

What to expect when the blood is sprinkled by faith - Hebrew11:28

- Preservation from the destroyer - *Hebrew11:28*
- The blood release people from bondage - *Exodus12:31-36*
- The blood brings defense - *Zachariah 9:15*
- The blood brings restoration – *Zachariah 9:11-12*
- The blood bring prosperity – *Exodus 12:36*
- The blood brings cleansing - *1John 1:7*
- The blood of Jesus purges – *Hebrew 9:14*

3. The Blood of drinking

For the purpose of this book, our focus will be on the drinking of the blood. As we have said earlier, we sprinkle the blood to deal with external evil forces but we drink the blood at the Holy Communion table to deal with internal forces and matters of our health; that is, the blood we drink at the Holy Communion table - the blood is served to us via the Holy Communion table.

So one of the ways to administer the blood of Jesus is by drinking it – *Matthew 26:27-29*.

The second element is the blood; what is in the blood or what does it contains? Apostle Paul refers to it as the cup of blessing *(1 Corinthians 10:16.)*. Blessing is the opposite of curse.

So drinking the blood is drinking blessing into your body.

What is in the blood?

Please note that the blood of Jesus did not come from a man it came from the Holy Spirit - *(Matthew 1:20)*. Therefore, inside his blood is the DNA of the Holy Spirit; so the blood contains the liquid force of the Holy Spirit for internal treatment. It is not ordinary which it is the life of Jesus *(Leviticus 17:11, 14)* in a sense. Consequently, when you are drinking his blood you are drinking the very naked life of Jesus and no sickness or disease can survive therein.

Blood is life *(Leviticus 17:14)*. Life is communicated via the blood. When the blood dries up life is ended; so drinking his blood is drinking his life. When Jesus offered us his blood he literally offered us his life that is why his blood is called the Blood of Redemption *Revelation 5:9*. You are redeemed from sin and sickness if you are drinking his blood at the Holy Communion table. You are drinking his life into your body. If you have the life of Jesus, then you have the health of Jesus flowing in you. I want you to have this revelation as you partake of the Holy Communion.

From Paul's writing, the Corinthians Christians had no problem in discerning or understanding the blood, but our generation does not have the understanding of both the body and the blood. The problem of the Corinthian Church was their inability to discern or understand the body of Jesus hence the Bible says that because they did not discern the Lord's body, many were sick *(1 Corinthians 11:29-30)*.

For our generation to enter and enjoy the blessedness of the Holy Communion we must understand the nutrients packed inside body and the blood of Jesus for our total health.

In whom we have redemption through his blood, the forgiveness of sins, according to the riches of his grace.
Ephesians 1:7

> *In whom we have redemption through his blood, even the forgiveness of sins.*
>
> **Colossians 1:14**

So, the blood factor brings about the forgiveness of sin and the body brings about the healing.

Benefits of Communion

1. It carries double cure

> *He brought them forth also with silver and gold: and there was not one feeble person among their tribes.*
>
> **Psalms 105:37**

Partaking of the Holy Communion opens the doors to health and wealth; double cure. Curing poverty and curing disease.

> *Bless the Lord, O my soul: and all that is within me, bless his holy name. Bless the Lord, O my soul, and forget not all his benefits: Who forgiveth all thine iniquities; who healeth all thy diseases.*
>
> **Psalm 103:1**

Forgiveness and healing go hand in hand as a double cure. Anywhere you see God forgiving people, healing takes place in the same place; that is why during any crusade when Altar call for sinners is made and the moment their sins are forgiven the next thing that happens is that the floodgates of healing miracles are flung open because the same blood that takes away sin takes away sickness.

It is an error for you to have righteousness operational in your soul through forgiven of your sins and have sickness and disease tormenting your flesh. That error must not continue in your life. I want you to be angry with that sickness in your body and use your new understanding to partake of the Holy Communion for your health by the force of faith.

So, you have double cure today in the blood of Jesus.

2. The power of proclaiming His death

For as often as ye eat this bread, and drink this cup, ye do shew the Lord's death till he come.
1 Corinthians 11:26

If you get this revelation today, it would give you some dimension of victory and liberty because you shall know the truth and the truth that you know not the one the pastor knows will make you free but the one you know is what makes you free.

The truth does not set free rather it makes free. Knowledge can turn you on the conqueror in you and make you say enough is enough. The enemy can only cheat you to the strength of your ignorant. The Bible says as often as you eat it you show the Lord's death till he comes. If that is so, why are we taking it occasionally? Some take it maybe once a week, others once a month or once in three months and you expect to see the miracles? No.

As often as you do this; partaking of the bread and drinking of the cup of blessing *(1 Corinthians 10:16)*. Who are you proclaiming the Lord's death to? Who are you showing the Lord's death to? Who is the Bible talking about?

> *And having spoiled principalities and powers, he made a shew of them openly, triumphing over them in it.*
>
> **Colossians 2:15**

We will spoil the enemy's business today. Every of their transaction in the village or wherever they are operating, we will spoil their business. We will spoil their plans.

What they have planned for you, your family, your children, business etc., today will be spoilt in Jesus name. Whenever you see a family and children tell you about their nightmare; anywhere demonic activities is taking place, take the Holy Communion and begin to proclaim the Lord's death over all powers of Hell.

If you notice, it was the Passover that the children of Israel partook of that proclaimed death of Pharaoh and the firstborn of every household in Egypt *(Exodus 12:29-32)*.

Until the judgment of death was proclaimed Pharaoh did not allow the children to go. When you partake of the Holy Communion with this understanding, the devil and his agents will flee; they will take to their heels. This is how to unleash the power of God in the Holy Communion. I once read this testimony, that, there was a house where a man was haunted. Haunted means you will see demonic movement. Demons will appear in a house and be moving or moving things. The pastor sent two of his members there; an elder and a deacon; they took the Holy Communion there based on this scripture, proclaiming the Lord's over every demonic activity in the house. That was the last day that oppression occurred.

As at the time of writing there are tenants now in the house; no devil went there anymore. So you can take Holy Communion for health and you can take it for warfare. When you are under any demonic attack go for it. Any satanic attack that you are suffering now cannot be compare to what Christ went through on the cross. Unleash the attack on the works of the devil in your life and you will see immediate results.

Are you moving to a new house, stepping into a new shop, take the Holy Communion; declare that you stand on the revelation of the word and proclaim the Lord's death on every works of the devil. The bible says take the Holy Communion *'till I come'* - that is how you should show the Lord's death till He comes.

Till He comes, your back must not be on the floor. It should not be said that the devil cheated you and successfully did it without repercussions. We must spoil the works of the devil by partaking of the Holy Communion.

Some people have no problem with their health but there are some issues they are dealing with; things on children; things that have to do with their mind, brain; you should take it consistently with them. It must be a consistent thing. The Bible says He broke the bread and their eyes were opened. It also affects you mentally. You have a mental access. You can reason faster.

The Bible says their understanding was opened

and they knew Him. You partake of the Holy Communion for mental open doors.

If you read something once or twice without understanding it, take the Holy Communion. You should not fail exams anymore as a believer. The Bible says that, in Jesus is hidden all wisdom and the knowledge of God. In other words, we use the Holy Communion to fight the enemy over the activities of principalities and powers. Proclaim the Lord's death over satanic activities in your affairs and declare the Lord's death over anything that is hindering you from succeeding.

Till He comes, declare your victory is guaranteed. No matter how stubborn the problem posed to be now, it would bow, in Jesus' name.

It was through this same mystery of the Passover that Judgment was proclaimed on the gods of Egypt *(Exodus 12:12)* that were backing Pharaoh's resistance to release the Jews from bondage. The mystery brings judgment both on the diabolical, wicked, invisible, and, visible forces.

If the blood of animals in Egypt could do that, how much more would the blood of Jesus do in your life.

I heard this testimony of a lady on the aircraft who had a blood clot while traveling to Israel with a sister. The blood clot moved from her leg to the brain and she then collapse and gave up. She was rushed to the hospital in Israel. When the Pastor heard about it, they had already put tube everywhere saying she will not survived it though she was still breathing but lifeless. The Pastor called her friend and said let's take the Holy Communion and proclaim her healing.

They were in their hotel room and took the Holy Communion as agreed, and began to proclaim her healing while she was in A&E. The following day, every organ that failed revived and the clot also that came from her leg to the brain disappeared. They did not have to be there. When the Lord was alive he had to physically to come to your place. He can only be in one place at a time but now that he is raised from the dead, he can be in ten places at the same time. His body can enter anywhere. He does not need any key. He can enter where they have tied your life down and say *'loose him and let him go'*. I don't know what has been tied down in your life, and you have been sensing its resistance, you are going to speak to that area.

> *The wind bloweth where it listeth, and thou hearest the sound thereof, but canst not tell whence it cometh, and whither it goeth: so is every one that is born of the Spirit.*
> **John 3:8**

You are not limited by location. You can speak to something in London, England anywhere. *The wind bloweth; does the wind need a visa? The wind bloweth; does it buy any ticket? The wind bloweth;* does it require pilot? The wind blows across continents. You can move on the strength of the wind of the Spirit and begin to deal with issues that are outside here and watch it change because you are speaking with a blood washed mouth. Your healing and deliverance are a blood bought right. It is your right.

3. It can reverse ageing

For you to be looking seventy years at forty, you need to look into that issue. The Holy Communion has a way of reversing ageing. When Adam sinned, God's judgment came on man and our body became subject to decay. Ageing process sets in. The more there is sin, the more the life span of man reduces. Divine judgment came on Adam. God says you will die if you take the forbidden fruit and when he did that, death process began. The first man that died was under age – Abel. Adam died at the age of nine hundred plus but today can you meet a nine hundred years old man?

The more sin, the more life span reduces. Divine judgment begins to work on man's body. Have you noticed that the more our generation moves faster in technology, the lower people life span? People now die at age forty, thirty, but in the bible days you would just be like those in primary school at this age and since ageing brings decay it also affects our brain cells because we start forgetting things as we grow older.

Holy Communion is the solution to us to offset this decay. How do I know? The Holy Communion helps in reversing ageing and helps you walk in divine health. That is what God meant when He talked about judgment in *(1 Corinthians 11:26)*.

He said when you eat and drink, you take judgment unto yourself,if it is taking wrongly. In other words divine judgment of not taking it correctly is what leads to sickness, weakness and death; because you take it unworthily and you therefore take death and judgment. That is what the Bible calls damnation. If you now take it correctly therefore, you take good health, strength and long life to yourself. It reverses the effect of ageing. The Holy Spirit helps you anytime you take the Holy Communion to reverse the effect of the curse of divine judgment to your body.

4. *Anti-death drug* - *John6:48-51*

Partaking of the flesh of Jesus which is the bread from heaven can terminate death. The communion therefore is an anti-death drug. It keeps death at bay in your life. If you partake of it daily, you are charging yourself up with divine life. As you partake of the Holy Communion, you are keeping every part of your body alive. This is one of the potencies of the Holy Communion.

Here we see Jesus showing us one of the nutritional values of the body compared to those that ate Manna in the wilderness but were died. As you partake of the flesh of Jesus, you will not die in the wilderness in your journey of life the way the Fathers died in the wilderness, because Divinity is entering your humanity. It is celestial body entering into a terrestrial body. No sickness and disease can survive inside the body of Jesus. So, as you partake of his body, it would swallow up that sickness like the rod of Moses swallowed up the rod of the magicians in Egypt.

5. Terminate satanic trickery plots-Mark14:1-2

When you sense a satanic conspiracy going on over your life or a plot calculated to take your life,then partake of communion regarded here as feast of Passover to terminate that plan,so you do not become a victim of negative imagination, because the bible says concerning Jesus the chief priest and the scribe could not carry that plan during the feast of Passover .

*Mark14:2.....*Not during the feast....

As long as you are partaking of the feast,you become an equation that is too difficult to solve for the devil,that plot could not work as long as you are partaking of the feast.

So the communion can bring deliverance for you trickery and negative imagination of people against you *(Acts12:11)*,which I call jokely wishes craft that is negative wishes that are crafted in the heart of men against you,this is a form of witchcraft.

Just as they could take Jesus by trickery,no devil would be to take out your life as you partake of this communion in Jesus Name.

6. Eyes opening miracles - Luke24:30-31,35

The manner in which Jesus broke bread revealed his identity to them - *Luke24:35*,their perception of Jesus went beyond mere physical recognition.

So partaking of this communion can open your mind to revelations of things that can reveal you to your world,that is show you things that would make you a show to your world. Partaking of the communion can open the eyes of your mind to things that are hidden to others,so as often as you partake of communion you, you increase your spiritual perception and comprehension of scripture *(Luke 24:45)*. Please note way you cannot perceive you cannot receive.

7. You draw strength, health and long life - 1Corinthians11:29-30

When you partake of this communion with understanding, expect to receive strength, health and long life.

You draw strength that can increase your life span *(Psalm90:10)*, the longer you want to live the more strength you need and that of kind of strength is available on the communion table and that is how it prolong your life.

CHAPTER 6
Testimonies

HEALING VIA THE HOLY COMMUNION.

"I am thanking God for what he did for me concerning my health. For some time now I have been having challenges with my health. I was having very serious body pains all over my body. I went to the hospital and I was given some very strong pain killers but those pain killers were not working at all. The pain was still there.

One day the pain came very strong that I couldn't stop crying. I called my husband to pray and prepare Holy Communion for me to take. After taking the Holy Communion I didn't know how I felt asleep till day break which was very impossible for me before even with the pain killers. With this experience I started to take the Holy Communion and anoint myself too. Ever since then the pain had gone, I haven't felt any pain and I have never stopped taking the Holy Communion daily too. I give all the glory to God and praise for my divine healing"

Sis. V.

MY PLACENTA ADJUSTED VIA THE HOLY COMMUNION.

"I want to thank God for his goodness in my life. When I was pregnant of my first daughter, I was told that my placenta was down and as a result, if it does not change I will have to give birth by caesarean operation. When I got home I started anointing my tummy and taking of the Holy Communion every day. To the glory of God, when I went back to run another test, the placenta had adjusted to the right place and I gave birth normally"

Deaconess T.

VICTORY THROUGH THE HOLY COMMUNION TABLE.

"I had a dream once where-in someone forced me to take a medication.

I woke up sick because of this experience. Few days after I observed that my skin started to develop pulse, which made me really sick, and because I work in the health sector, I was not allowed to work because of my health state in order not to affect others.

So this attack was now moving from

my dream to my physical health and now to my work which invariably would affect my finances. I called Pastor Adebo and explained my ordeal to him

He prayed and ministered the Holy Communion to me and the yoke of the enemy was broken immediately. Hallelujah!"

Elder (Mrs) B.

2016 BREAK OUT MANDATE TO WASHINGTON.D.C USA

The Holy Spirit gave an instruction for go to Washington D.C. USA to kick start the operation of this ministry with a Healing and miracles summit and in obedience we schedule the program for *9-10th July 2016*, even I have never step Washington D.C. in my entire life but the Lord went with me and showed up on the meeting with healing in his wings, the ground breaking ministration was successful with testimonies below and as am writing this book am in the way back to Washington D.C. for the second edition of this bimonthly program.

So if you are within this Area of Washington D.C. come and be a part of this great move of the Holy Spirit, contact us today by calling the line on the handbill or email me:

info@destinychurchnations.org

Visit my Facebook Page: Destiny Church for all Nations
YouTube Channel: Pastor Adebo Tomomewo

Highlights of the Destiny church for all nations international Washington D.C, this ground work began in 8th July 2016, in obedience to the voice of the Holy Spirit, see what the lord has done in 3months, Glory to God

Testimonies

INSTANT HEALING OF 5yrs ARTHRITIS

Praise the Lord Pastor Adebo, this is a long overdue healing testimony of God's healing power on July 15, 2016

My dear sister Coach Wanda left a message on my phone, about you Pastor, coming to DC holding a Healing and Miracle Service July 15-16, 2016.

I heard the message on the early morning of the 15th. I heard the Spirit of God say, "Go to this meeting." I don't usually go to a lot of meetings, because I attend a strong Spirit Filled Ministry and I receive from God answers to prayer, healing, so only if I hear clearly from the Lord do I attend other meetings.

Well I knew it was God so I called Wanda and told her I would be there. Got the address and planned my day so I would be free to get to this meeting.

When I reached the building, there was

a parking space in front. I just rejoiced!

It's not always parking in DC near your destination.

I looked at the building and there was a stairway that was so steep and many steps. I HAD arthritis in my right knee so painful that I hesitated and looked around the building for a ramp. I didn't look forward to actually walking up those steps. No ramp.... so I just said Lord help me get up these steps.

Praise the Lord, I walked up those steps with very little difficulty. I said, Lord you have already started the healing! I entered the building with great expectation. When I got in and took my seat, you were already ministering. Just as I got settled in my seat you said something to this effect, "the presence of God is already in this room. Healing is in this room. I may not lay my hands or touch you and you will be healed. " I could discern His presence. The Spirit of God was all in the room.

You began to call out certain ailments. When you called for people with arthritis, I came. I think others came up also. I told you I had arthritis in my knee or about 5 years. Your prayed for me and I felt the Spirit of God take over and I was on the floor engulfed in His presence.

When I stood up there was absolutely <u>NO PAIN IN MY KNEE. NONE WHAT SOEVER.</u>

I know you spoke to me before I went to my seat, I just don't remember what you said

When I got back to my seat, I heard the Lord say to me," Now that you have received your healing you have to be reminded how to keep it." When you finished ministering to people, you came back to speak to us all. This is what you said, "Now that I will tell you how to keep your healing." Then you told us how.

I went to my church that Sunday and I gave this testimony. I have been telling everyone I know and some I didn't know.

I thank God that I recognize His Voice and was obedient to what He said that day. Today I am healed and strong in the Lord and in the power of HIS might.

Thank you Pastor, for also being obedient to come to the US! We needed to hear all you said to us! I am encouraged and challenged by your message to us. May God's mighty hand continue to be on you as you continue to follow His lead.

Serving in Joy,
Pastor (Pat)

I FELT DIFFERENT

I felt different when I saw people getting healed on July 9, 2016. My left hand is what God uses. Thank you Jesus for Restoring the Healing gift in my Left hand. When Pastor Adebo spoke restoration for me I know it had to be God speaking. I had not been used in years to lay hands on people and to speak healing over the phone or in person. The heat and power of God manifests and God uses me as a conduit for the power. Pastor Adebo said it is a restoration of God's using me to lay hands on people and speak God's healing. I can't heal a fly or a flea. It is God using me. God has used me multiple times as a channel of His healing. I give God the Glory. Pastor Adebo spoke strength. He said I would leave the meeting laughing and smiling and that I won't go out the same as I came in. I was crying when I came in and I was lifted up as I left.

Sis.R

HEALED OF ARTHRITIS

I was more than delighted to attend the meeting on July 9, 2016. I was miraculously healed of arthritis. I can walk better and am going up and down stairs without any pain. I am getting better day by day. My soul was touched. I am believing God for total healing in my body. Thank God for Pastor Adebo's coming to the city. I am looking forward to more things happening for our children and neighbours

Minister S.

The handbill of this programs can be seen below. You are next on line for a miracles.

YOU ARE INVITED!

If the testimony of Destiny Church for all Nations and the work among the homeless community in London has inspired you, and you want to witness the outreach first - hand, our team will be glad to welcome you!

Visit us at any of these times:

<u>Sunday Services</u>
1st Service (Jesus Breakfast) — 9:00am
2nd Service — 10:30am
<u>Monday Service</u>
Recovery Class —7:00pm
<u>Wednesday Service</u>
Hour of Destiny teaching and communion service —7:00pm
<u>Friday Service</u>
Prevailing Prayer force —7:00pm
<u>Last Friday of the Month</u>
London Holy Ghost Night —11.00pm

Find venue details on our website
www.destinychurchnations.org

DO YOU WANT TO LEARN MORE?

You can now order for the DVD tagged:

TAKING THE CHURCH BEYOND THE WALLS & TESTIMONIES OF TRANSFORMATION

Learn how we started this feeding project with 10 homeless men, and how we are now feeding over 200 people every week.
You can order for this material from the address below.

Are you a pastor or ministry leader? Do you want us to train and mobilise your people on how to take the church beyond the walls?

Please contact us through the following:
Outreach coordinator
(+44)7950950815
You can also send an e-mail to:
info@destinychurchnations.org

BOOK SHELF

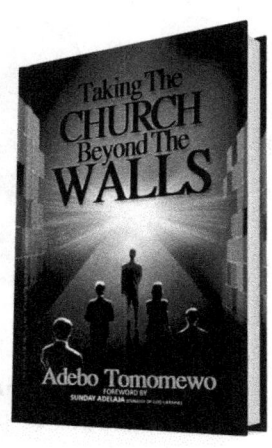

Taking the Church Beyond the Walls is a testimony of how Destiny Church for All Nations (London), under the leadership of Pastor Adebo, has succeeded in converting the revelation of the gospel of the Kingdom, as taught by pastor Sunday Adelaja, into visible and tangible results. It is full of practical wisdom and ideas that can inspire readers to become more relevant in their communities.

The Role of the Supernatural is a follow-up to *Taking the Church Beyond the Walls*, the documented testimony of how Destiny Church for all Nations, London, under the leadership of Pastor Adebo & Hyelazira Tomomewo began to reach out to the homeless in the heart of London. It shows the important role the Holy Spirit in converting the gospel of the Kingdom into visible and tangible result. Full practical wisdom to become more relevant in their respective communities.

Your destiny is a journey. Every day you are either walking within your destiny or walking away from it. Destiny is what everybody is born with but is coded. It is your birth right yo decode your destiny that is veiled in a mystery or hidden away and, once found, fulfil it with God's help. When you are born with a destiny it means you are born with a purpose.

This book will teach you how to find, follow and fulfil it.

This teaching series primarily addresses why fail to achieve their vision. Through divine revelation of Gods word, Pastor Adebo Tomomewo uncovers the true reasons why people fail to accomplish their God given vision.

This teaching covers:
- Why people finish halfway
- Understanding the place of vision
- Prophetic words for finishing strong
- 5 things you inherit through the Abrahamic covenant

The foremost reason why bad things happen to good people is ignorance. The Devil's greater weapon is ignorance. You can fight a battle you don't know exist.

In this teaching, the Lord will send His light into the dark areas of your life and expose the hidden sources of your troubles.

This teaching covers:
- How to discern between clean and unclean
- Blocking Satan's legal ground to your life
- Recognising accursed things as sources of hidden trouble
- Confronting the Devils in your bloodline 1&2

The picture here shows our impact in the community, you see our members reaching out to the elderly during Christmas, testimonies of transformation being shared by those that attend the breakfast service on one of pastor Adebo outings. Tuesday personal development discipleship class with Sis.Anna Atu and the table set for their dinner, pupils of supplementary school at the inaugural day of the school In April 2009.

Support Logo given us in acknowledgement of community impact, by Southwark borough council of London England.

This picture show the first service of Recovery chapel London, our kitchen runs, called Jesus breakfast service that started with 10 people from the street of London been served full English breakfast, it has grown to become our first service today, within the auditorium we seen 200 people, this breakfast take place every Sunday 9:00am to the homeless, rough sleepers and the hungry, over 1000 homeless has visited our feeding project every Sunday in the city of London. Come and see lives of people being radically changed as they hear the gospel of the kingdom while eating their breakfast.

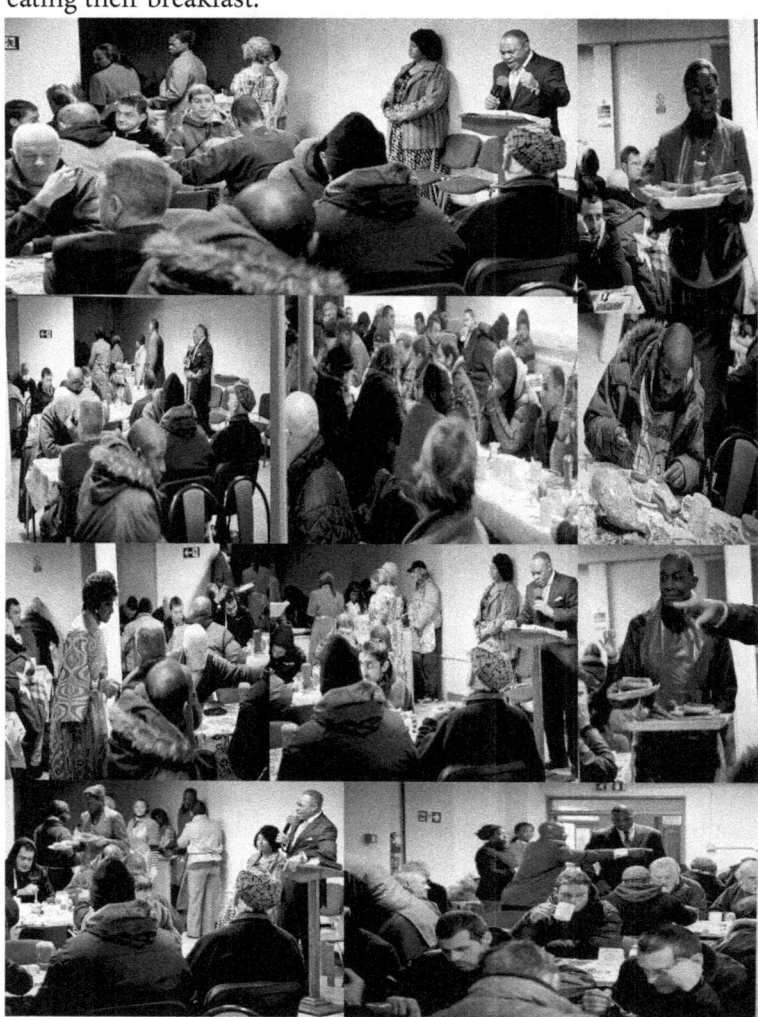

1. Pastor Adebo at History makers training in Kiev Ukraine
2. Pastor Adebo after a ministration in Vienna Austria
3. Pastor Adebo after ministering in Kiev Ukraine

1. Pastor Adebo, when invited to the house of commons July 2011; 2. Pastor Adebo with Governor Olusegun Agagu, Ondo state in Akure Nigeria 2006.; 3. Pastor Adebo with Former Nigerian Head of state ,General Yakubu Gowon.; 4. Pastor Adebo in Downing street, poising for a snap shot with other delegates at the prime minister door, Whitehall London England.; 5. Pastor Adebo with Former Mayor of London, Ken livingstone.2010; 6. Pastor Adebo with the present Mayor Boris Johnson 2011; 7. Pastor Adebo with Valerie Shawcross. London Assembly member for the borough Lambeth and Southwark.; (This pictures explain the chapter that deals with the church with influence)

1. Pastor Adebo with pastor Sunday Adelaja and Apostle Alfred Williams; 2. Pastor Adebo with pastor.W.F.Kumuyi and his wife; 3. Pastor Adebo with pastor Mike Tomomewo at the edge; 4. Pastor Adebo with pastor Natalya Potopayeva in Frankfurt Germany; 5. Pastor Adebo with Apostle Tuff and his wife; 6. Pastor Adebo,Bishop Jide Orire, pastor(Mrs)Stella and others; 7. Pastor Adebo and pastor Andy hawthorn of The message Trust at house of commons; 8. Pastor Adebo with bishop Wayne Malcolm at house of commons; 9. Pastor Adebo, Bishop Nelson, Dr.Agbeyomi from Altanta USA, Late Mayor Tayo Situ and wife

Pastor Adebo and his wife pastor (Mrs) Hyelazira Tomomewo along with three children David, Elijah and Princess

In this picture, we have the members of Recovery chapel International London in the second service. These are history makers; they made the vision of taking the beyond the wall possible. There kingdom commitment birthed it.

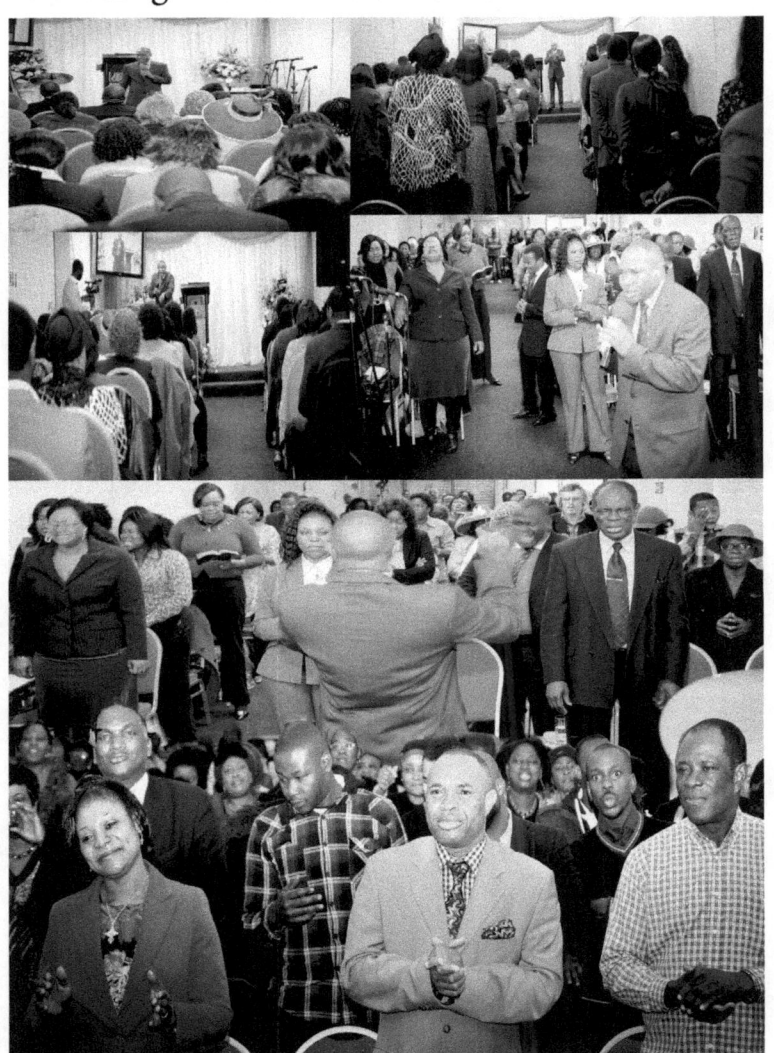

www.ingramcontent.com/pod-product-compliance
Lightning Source LLC
Chambersburg PA
CBHW071746040426
42446CB00012B/2488